QUESTIONS ABOUT CIRCULATION

CHARLES MALONE

DRIFTWOOD
PRESS

Independently published by *Driftwood Press*
in the United States of America.

Managing Poetry Editor: Jerrod Schwarz
Front & Back Cover Image: Nathaniel Saint Amour
Cover Design: Sally Franckowiak
Interior Design & Copyeditor: James McNulty
Fonts: Existence, Sitka, Garamond,
& Merriweather

Copyright © 2019 by Charles Malone
All Rights Reserved.

No part of this publication
may be reproduced, stored in a retrieval
program, or transmitted, in any form or by
any means (electronic, mechanical,
photographic, recording, etc.), without
the publisher's written permission.

First published in March 2019
ISBN-13: 978-1-949-06503-9

Please visit our website at www.driftwoodpress.com
or email us at editor@driftwoodpress.net.

PRAISE FOR
QUESTIONS ABOUT CIRCULATION

"*Questions About Circulation* is vivid and visceral and palpable. All the perks of James Wright and Wendell Berry, and lyricism all his own. The work is somehow softly abrasive."

— Erica Dawson,
author of *When Rap Spoke Straight to God*

"How to extract 'wonder from sediment,' especially if the sediment is vaguely toxic? This is the central question of Charles Malone's *Questions About Circulation*. One answer is to dig—the literal trace of land use, the lateral spread of material history, the billowing field of childhood memory. These poems brim with glacial moraine, crumbling mills, wild blackberry thickets, and 'a big peaceful cement pond [reflecting] tarnished copper.' But it is aftermath that concerns the present, and these poems haunt the body's arterial connections: 'a vein is a way elsewhere, and part of a circuit.' Tracing our entanglements, Charles Malone's *Questions About Circulation* returns us to the ground of our senses: 'and slow down/put the o in close the boy has flown.'"

— Matthew Cooperman,
author of *Spool*

Contents

Sharon Conglomerate	1
ruins	2
prelude	5
inside closed curves / logical relations	7
illusive / weeded	9
city a chorus	10
bus number four	11
bootstraps / gooseberries	12
callous	14
syrup	16
homing	17
One Dozen Frozen Ponds	18
Of the Nature of the Specified Thing	19
The Weight of Blooming	20
the house fire	21
Sap	22
...no farther, this is the place...	23
...the circuit is not closed, it is a fountain of energy...	24
...we are remodelling the Alhambra with a steam-shovel...	25
...I am thankful that this pond was made deep and pure for a symbol...	26
...not until we have lost the world...	27
Questions about Circulation	28
Interview	31

Sharon Conglomerate

Wonder from sediment
pull, call, dig
from time and place
to cochlea
& optic nerve
below the sod
to scent
to swerve thought
never only dirt
basalt, limestone
sharon conglomerate
eyes can almost feel
this is not synesthesia
it is a memory
I was losing
& who was she
walking from her small town
among lily of the valley
to the river bank
a knife
dull quartz
like stars quieted
by the lake

r u i n s

I.

Like Herculaneum, an unlikely artifact
in dark glacial Great Lake soil
something fired, something rusted.
Us boys play the Whetherills, little Percy Fawcetts.
We trace the edge of a lost building
in a thicket of prickers
in the woods we had to ourselves.
You find the carcass of a piano,
I find a scar waiting on a rusted nail,
a slash of light through shifting beech leaves.
And we glimpse the great before-us,
before the tulip trees, before the walls came down—
a cottage and a sugar house.
Once, where there was a frame to hold a door, the world
opens just for a moment we see the work of it, clearing
and sugaring—time slips away
takes a generation's work with it.
There is no equilibrium between the numbers
of ruined and ruining sugar houses.
Do you remember how big the woods felt?

II.

A summer baling hay, a spring break gathering sap.
I remember how heavy the buckets get as we pour
and pour, tight in shoulders and knuckles and knees.
Near freezing sap spills down my front
into my rubber boot
& in the sugar house the sweet steam erases
& in the sugar house I remember field trips, festivals
think college thoughts
think the old man might not have many more winters
think this way of life is dying.
& in the sugar house these thoughts profane
every muscle knows
every bright breath saccharine.

III.

The kitchen ceiling falls to the floor—
soaked plaster, moldy wood.
Hundred-year-old floors warp
something more sinister than time
in the farmhouse.
Plants grow to cover the windows,
the smell chokes
a massive colony of honeybees takes up in the siding,
raccoons come and go from the basement window.

This is the process by which a home becomes not,
a process other than a real estate transaction—
spills, arguments, accidents, cruelties.
You see other farmhouses stripped of paint
ducking behind wilding shrubs and flowering weeds.
The boundary between in and out blurs,
a sign with shameful orange letters on the door.
What action and inaction, what ruins a house
for the body and the lungs and recollection?
Rain, the creep of ivy, the sedimentary accumulation of dirt
this is the opposite of the joy of work.

p r e l u d e

I.

open   to an open boy in a farm's open field—
black soil
lead paint
a carriage stone
& a bell

all the rectangles of hay stacked dry & neat in the red barn
the grass is cut & the garage is full of tools

like the horizon
everything is rain-slick & operational

II.

the boy tears photos from the encyclopedia
finds an old city
        paris or
       prague etched or
      a castle a museum a cathedral
an old world away   —   chews, swallows it

in the top field his father bales hay with other sweating farmers
it is clear glaciers left them everything they need

wind smelling warm with cut grass stirs curtains in one round room

 grandma plays Beethoven on the grand

the piano says *need is a thin, prideful jacket*

listening, like dreaming he does not think
of his lost chance to sprint through timothy and alfalfa

inside closed curves / logical relations

I.

the newly agreed upon Reaganite future is shiny
        & not this
the newly agreed upon future of the family is not
        nuclear/(unclear)

grass will not be mowed regularly
the roof of the garage will sway, buckle, & bury

forget the future tense
   right now it's the 80s

        the children are exceptional
        the sweet corn is delicious
        each new round cul-de-sac is a nod
        to the first big red O in Ohio

II.

two ways of life overlap—venn circles

the space shared is purposefully sterile, suburban

one of the circles floats otherly
a lifesaver

ocean is alcohol
       pickups
       boredom

illusive / weeded

white chicken feathers scatter across the lawn
red specks glisten
                illusive & weeded
wet grass thick with dandelions.

        the door to the coop is ajar.

(beyond this) flight—the unguilty fox
a whitetail excited boy

into thick rows of pine,
                old limbs scratch & snap

                      coursing body slows
deeper in the woods
skittish deer bed down
& buckets rust
within the rectangle of a toppled sugarhouse

pick up a brick — the wet
rotting leaf smell it holds down rises
in hands, a cold mass

an earthworm writhes in the vacancy
reddish centipedes scatter

a potato bug rolls in the palm

city a chorus

beyond this—Cleveland
its methane flame burning in the flats

        El Greco's *Christ on the Cross*
hangs
outside constant construction fights to keep pace with decay
a big peaceful cement pond reflects tarnished copper
the Methodists' oil-can church

& escalators carry
families
        business & homeless men & women up
            into the marble belly of a tower

& all the streets and towers light up for show and safety
    in sounding night
      city is a chorus of sirens

& glass doors hold back stale, humid air
      worse when wind blows off the shallow lake
      where old shipwrecks
make drunk stories and craft beer labels

& seagulls chase garbage trucks
      warm currents
 exhaust lifts their wings

bus number four

hum endless motor om and jostle

contemplate the two Os in Ohio
    (their points of overlap occur in our living room and pantry
     in posters on bedroom walls, on cassettes and CDs, clothing,
    in and between the family)
I can't quite laugh at the kind greeting between them

like a camera's shutter
a clock-strike
a set-bound clapperboard claps

dirty hinged doors open and close
announcing arrivals, framing the day

the school bus shudders towards dawn, towards
the next kid, the next

clap/action and the boy, I remember
    wants to fix, doctor, & dream

& leave even the overlap for something pure

some brass jazz in some poor light, some lie
some library

bootstraps / gooseberries

I.

some country kids talk about escape, some don't
& some see the city a siren
        all those blue-grey eyes asking

every TV show is a travel agent selling

home becomes a choice
& the orchard might not be a long-term investment

        after all
we must distinguish ourselves

this is the message of the school newsletters
the announcements in the paper
each teacher's encouragement is a contract

or it isn't and never was

they don't say homestead or sustain
callous or tomato

proudly in American history "bootstraps"
"get out" they whisper

II.

a row of locust trees will become fence posts that won't rot
& this is generational thinking

after
there is a room filled to the ceiling with fresh sawdust

on one side flanked
a prickly thicket of blackberry
above by mud daubers,
& their pan flute nests

a brother burrows, a sister buries
in the warm wood shavings
        guarded
from sound & sight
born in dusk & dark we come up gasping

greeted again by light
& steam rising from the waste pile

we sell horse manure to fertilize lawns in the suburbs
& this is economical thinking

we pay for college with the mowing

c a l l o u s

I.

I cling to my growing fear of these dumbing hands
& every dirty, damp, rusty thing
every blossoming, rotting smell and taste

all this turns to love in a blister, burn, break, & blood-free arc toward memory

> browning apples
> sweet tendrils of grapevine
> the cicada scent of summer
> pine tar & maple sap

I feel at least two desires at once
this beautiful fractured family sits around
a round wooden picnic table

in order to not disappoint them
I'll come back and spread the ashes over the milkweed and trefoil

II.

all the old tools have wooden handles
smooth, not unsplit
they tear at your hands until your hands are better
you can grip them and feel your forearm's potential
you can drive the implement into history
dig, peel then peak back under the city
& brush the dried mud from your pant cuffs

disrepair, disinterest, & this list of reasons:
some great arc of storytelling in the history of the country
some fundamental flaw in the boy

naiveté pairs with an earnest need to be earnest
and pleasing or

indistinct, unexceptional, empty-handed

s y r u p

beyond these thoughts: everyone else—
the diner full of big bellied bearded men
all knuckles, deliberate gazes, and laughter
who between syrup splashes and coffee refills
say nothing and everything about spheres within spheres

I could grow dirty and strong
        a seed preserver, a designated exploitee
plant a small orchard and hybridize generations of apples
            a pumpkin patch
            a roadside stand
            heirloom tomatoes

            find some ecstatic vocabulary
all verbs and nouns   for a third circle
to run like a disc plow through our poetry
flip over narratives
        about manliness and pig shit
            rusted tangles of thought and work

and slow down

put the o in close the boy has flown

h o m i n g

not a dovecote or columbarium,
although I do like saying

"columbarium" and all of its unfolding wings

meaning "the pigeon shed behind the shop"

meaning home

It is in the first few weeks of life that they develop a sense of home. Here, they will always return. Transported blind. Scientists wonder what sense guides them. Run experiments. Write magnetic theories.

home becomes an action word

carriers a noun, the plastic latch release
unfolding wings unleashed

a few fast circles
climb, altitude
sensing a direction

meaning home

Breeders have an old con. If you don't know birds they'll sell you a mature one, one already homed. It will home, and you will be out a few hundred.

One Dozen Frozen Ponds

Three kids ring the white pondering the designs of water.
In time, the beautiful girl will find out she is beautiful
the troubled golden boy will find out he is troubled
the third is the last to follow across the ice.
He hears warning echo in bone and falls through.

Millions of boys must fall through frozen ponds
they freeze and become non-persons filling up
the space below the ice but above the water—

instant thaw clean ice to algae bloom
        solid then soup

to you through the ice golden and beautiful
troubled and knowing

        mothers to strip us down to long johns
and worry us warm in the tub
        and then gone

woven clove grove fro froguth zen muslin doe plimb would bracken burnt bough
bow oxen was bought own wonder wanter well wood wild coarse coursing curse

into a gasp of feathers

Of the Nature of the Specified Thing

You are not the solitary heron
or the fish in its beak.
You are not the morning mist
hovering over the face of the water
lit with all the colors of the fall.
You might be the smell of a century
of industry rich with iron
like blood, but your running
stretches farther than our history
of dragging canoes over the banks.
You are not your shape on the map
or the fires or the ore boats.
You are not round, not a circle
or the whisper of cattails
in the abandoned meander.
Sinuous does not share a root with sinew.
But you are the curve and connection
the random tendon pathfinding—
Geographers use the word stochastic
which means both to aim at and to guess.
But you are not a mouthful of words
I've aimed and missed while you've turned
the mill
carved the sandstone, recreated
cleaned us and absorbed
Furnace Run and Harper Ditch
and when I walk home at a loss
I see a single Heron stalk your banks
and a boy fish with his father
and spotfin shiners skirt in your cool pools.

The Weight of Blooming

The garden is tired of carrying the weight of blooming.
Stems bend, the unshot doe strips limbs from the apple tree,
mice burrow into the wall for warmth,
moles attack grubs in their dark tunnels
marking the grass with their passing.
Some of the apples are wormy
the deer piss and shit on them.
We must climb for clean fruit
the body is capable of so much living.
Can you imagine tunneling tireless in the dark?
Look for protein in the vulnerable larvae of an Asian beetle,
congregate in a great dark cathedral and murmur.
Dirt under the nails
surprising muscles pile strength in a hump on the back.
Determine to never heed our own soft bellies
or turn our dim gaze in.
Repetition. Defense. Words claw—
a narrow love buried
safe—false poverties of the mind.
We're doing it all wrong, poisoning our future.
The river is tired of carrying the waste of the bloom
can we give back the choices the map makers made
their armies sent out to push colored lines
and languages slammed against faith and surveying equipment,
to make fortunes and churches and others.
Where was a world before,
how many americas,
not underneath,
but like the body on acetate overlays
all present
astounding each other with capability.
Reacting birds shoot into flight
the deer's white flag
more Maslow than Pizarro.

the house fire

methane cuts through water
a rising bubble, an earth aneurysm
as we quake the fire out
and heat and eat and winter
and pave and pave
so the kids can drive off
to bigger and bigger cities

then, like a waterfall reversed
and powering up into the night sky
everything converts to light
the force of the explosion shakes the school
the middle school concert band hesitates, continues

burnt pages floating on the surface of an irrigation pond
a farmer's library, a house full of flammable
shredded and reassembled by accident
tiny scraps, individual words, pieces of letters
the strangest precipitation

Sap

The orchard is wild and brittle;
the ground is covered in brown apples.
Between the thumb and forefinger
dusky softness under the skin—discomfort/squirm.
Something is happening to the sugar bush;
the old trees are dropping limbs.
I know I am drunk on autumn and nostalgia
so I hesitate to say anything at all.
The ground freezes and thaws and freezes.
I climb into the fork of familiar branches
I sling a rope over a pulley to haul up the library
and nest in the thoughts of worldly people.
They are warm and smell like hay.
I borrow borrow borrow and shiver at night
and share all my worries with the dark.

...no farther, this is the place...

I tell myself coming home is part of the natural order
like I'm a damn pigeon.

I walk through the forest, the abandoned farm—wildflowers throat deep.
I tell you I love this landscape, it is comfortable.

We sink into intricacy: moss, red caps
the skin of a garter, the pelt of a rabbit.
Texture, pattern, gradient.

I long for the other places I've lived
split nature, cross purposes, mountains, canyons—

love is a governor
bathed in the unsteady light of October.

I want to walk until we are muddy
out of breath, and thirsty to the point of worry
then go home to roost and coo.

> ...the circuit is not closed,
> it is a fountain of energy...

We take a break from the haymaking
sweat beads and runs. A line of trees
separates this field from the next. In their shade

I scrape my forearm, a knot of old black barbed-wire
a red globe shines, darkens and shrivels.
I notice the tap wound on one of the maples,
I see a spruce that's dropped lower limbs—
a round wound, white crust over amber.

Is this nostalgia, soaking in the sweet,
sun flowing in the visceral cavities of reminiscence?
It's sappy and syrupy, diluted and not good for us
Is the labor of poetry ever accurate enough?

I don't do this work anymore and
I don't go in the old house if I can help it.

> ...we are remodeling the Alhambra
> with a steam-shovel...

I buy another old house as a stand-in for the one we lost.
I try to save it. We try to save it together—
rip up the carpet, tacks bite bodies, staples,
the smell of piss and the dust of other's skin.
I kick and haul and am down on the floor like an animal
after screws and nails trying to bring it back to life.
They are up on the roof of memory, shingles rain down,
They are painting the wet basement and the walls upstairs,
They are hive, they are time sped up and backwards.

There is some concrete image of *finished* not unlike
the place I grew out of—what is this psychology?

A chrysalis on the underside of the broad milkweed leaf in a yellow field.

Each evening we sit panting, heaving on the front steps
beer, a glass of wine, no furniture, proud.
The work will ever be done.

> ...I am thankful that this pond was
> made deep and pure for a symbol...

A rainbow sheens on the water
some light penetrates, some reflects, some bends.

When your feet sink into the fine, cool mud
you smell the distinct odor of natural gas.
You get water and grit in your eye.

Every house on the street has a rusty well.
The company sold the rights to another company
the lease yellows in a drawer of an old oak desk.

Writhing tadpoles wreath the pond
this was a charmed childhood, of course
because it is the one that I remember.

I can already hear the late summer nights ahead,
frog song and the nudge—*go out and play.*

I see an auction sign at the farm on the corner.
Rotting round bales and a broken haybine,
manure and mud splashed on the white walls.
I worry about this way of life that I never lived.

I can't help the thought, I am getting old.
Slipping from revolution to reaction, rusting.
I feel it in my joints.

I hold a crisp cicada skin between my fingers.

...not until we have lost the world...

I have felt good dimensions of loss,
but this is not it.
Not just farms, but boys
loose in the woods, bolting
across pastures, pressing gooseberries
between their fingers just for surprise
the moment of burst
when the tension is too much
and there is no going back.

Except where the deer maintain them,
the trails narrow and fade.
The woods are so quiet now.

Questions About Circulation

1. A mouth over our mouth. Nose pinched, someone else's idea of breath opening our chest. Wet warm molecules in disarray — a long line of wanderers.

2. A generous teacher invites us into his home. Anchored by polio, he tells us he travels widely within these walls. In response to some needy and earnest thing one of us says, he observes that it takes seven years to know a place. His whole being is breath and season.

3. Each year beyond seven we grow more used to our own bullshit. Lawn decorations, new wall colors, sloppy thinking. Some specific thing arrested.

4. After diverting, seemingly halting, the river with coffers workers depose the old dam. The concrete despot. The river bottom naked, littered, stinking. The sawmills are long gone, like the trees worth harvesting. We come back to flow and fish — to recreate. A better state. I declare it a return but worry it could be a cycle, like so many things. Can a river know roundness and can we say we have made something better when the timeline is so long?

5. We have been walking a long time. Teeth bite delicate tree-shaped wood sorrel and release sweetness. Chew the delicate pink tendrils of grape vines. Eyes seek wild fruit and a source of water. With each breath we try to smell the cool creek. We have been walking for generations.

6. You pack and unpack your home. Are you really wandering if you bring your books everywhere you go? Are you wandering if you walk without stopping to read? Are books anchors or catapults? You say you are fairly certain words get into the blood but cannot be detected by mass spectrometry. When you open the box of books the whole room begins to smell like you.

7. We tax and dig and build. A forgotten arm of the river is buried under the streets. It rushes icy and black and pretends to pulse from a heart the size of a garage. Home among the great stone foundations, I-beams and rebar. The covering roads built to allow movement are choked.

8. Two things: A vein is a way elsewhere and part of a circuit. Libraries archive a thousand ways elsewhere; when they work properly the books come back.

9. In fact, we cross the great plains alone, or in the smallest groups. Out and returning to the last breath blossoming in a black rattling flower and twenty shadows of ourselves from every Christmas before movement forced our lives out of our childlike chrysalises. The first house of memory.

10. Owning a home. A foundation grasping at the surface of the earth. A sandy hilltop, glacial clay, the shore of the draining river. The flooding river: abundance and scarcity — a long, slow breath opening our chest warm and wanting oxygen. Choked like an algae bloom. Like beetle kill. A triumphant fistful of wild carrots.

11. A long line of wanderers coming to rest spiteful of the long line of wanderers yet to come to rest. Taxing the land we love. Forcing arrest. All us little live things stumbling into community, with its consequences.

A RIVER WITH QUICK, DARK WATERS
a conversation with
Charles Malone & Jerrod Schwarz

Questions About Circulation **occupies an interesting intersection of geography and childhood. In your own words, how do these two elements inform each other in the collection?**

I am from rural Northeast Ohio and went to college just down the road. When manufacturing jobs left, people left. If you grow up in the orbit of a city like Cleveland, or Detroit, or Pittsburgh in a period of decline, it is possible to both be aware of the great things about these places and also feel how they struggle to redefine themselves. I don't think I understood the place or the people until I'd lived elsewhere. In my twenties, I ached not for a bigger city but a different landscape. This led me to follow the midwestern tradition of heading west. When I arrived in booming Fort Collins—not irrelevantly named for a man who had lived in Ohio and served in the State Senate before heading to Colorado—I had to get used to a culture and mindset of growth and progress just as I had to get used to the altitude and sunshine.

One of my first poetry teachers in Kent, Maj Ragain, said it takes seven years to come to know a place. As I got to know the cycles of the rivers and mountains, the crush of tourists, the smothering summer heat and wildfires, and the pressures that a booming populations puts on the land and the community, I also better understood my home state. I knew intimately the aspirational landscape of the Rocky Mountains and the moodier farms and watersheds of the Great Lakes. Eventually, I came back home. It surprised me that my journey became a circuit instead of an arc; I had to make sense of that narrative. In a way, my desire to see different geographies helped me understand the place and the people that shaped my childhood.

I'm also a slow writer and editor. It takes me time to understand my work on a manuscript level. It takes me time to light up my blind spots. Because I'm slow, I'd travelled across the country and back before these poems found their final forms and found their relationships to one another. It was in my last year of living in Colorado when the bulk of this manuscript emerged as one long poem about growing up in Ohio. It wasn't until I came back to the Midwest that I could see the bigger questions behind the poems and the parts of the manuscript that were holding it back.

There is wonderful and striking rural imagery littered throughout these poems. In your own words, what are the advantages of writing poems set against a pastoral backdrop?

I'm glad you feel the heart of those images. If there was an advantage to drawing on this rural landscape it was that I felt a responsibility not to let these poems be just one thing. In other words, my fear of recreating the fallacies that undermine pastoral writing was what drove me to work and rework these poems. If they were quiet, beautiful, and simplistic, they would be dishonest. If I treated the farmers I knew the way Patrick Kavanagh treats his farmer, Maguire, in the "The Great Hunger"—how he uses Maguire's ignorant and stunted-self to cut against characterizations of the rural life in Ireland, I would also be ignoring the joy I found in being close to the land and in hard, physical work. Instead, I try to invite the reader's bodies into the poems. I try to allow complexity into them. I've tried not to write easy poems.

If I am really honest, to an extent I didn't have a choice. Once I made the choice to write seriously, the backdrop I was born into was the backdrop I had to work with. Along the way I made other choices to try to understand the systems and attitudes that shape our relationship with the land and approaches to agriculture. I had a number of odd outdoor jobs out west: pigeon wrangler/photographer for a rafting company, mosquito control technician, and I'd had a working membership with a small community-supported farm. I like hard work. The accomplishments of writing can be so hard to measure, but you know when you are done moving a pile of stone or harvesting a row of beets. I did this partly to understand where I came from and partly because I get restless under fluorescent lights. I also believe the pastoral holds clues to understanding better ways of living in relationship with the land. Our ecological crisis has its roots and its solutions here.

On the whole though, I've struggled a lot with this imagery. Sometimes it is beautiful, sometimes bloody. The pastoral mode has problems, we've been trying to reinvent it for generations. We can't shake it, and we haven't figured out how to fix it. By luck, or by library, I found that growing up in a rural place did not prevent me from accessing our best cultural creations. I also found that not everyone cultivated their curiosity they way they cultivated their crops and livestock. Like many writers, I always felt a little bit at odds with my hometown. Having Cleveland nearby is special for someone looking to grasp the larger world; it has a world-class art museum that is always free to the public, one of the best Orchestras in the country, and great universities. The combination of rich soil and incredible art can make for a good childhood if you take advantage of both.

How long had you been working on this collection? What poems, structures, or ideas didn't make it into the final manuscript, and why were they cut?

I've been working on this collection since I started taking myself seriously as a poet. The oldest poem in here, "Homing," I wrote after a summer working as a photographer with a white-water rafting company in 2007. We used homing pigeons to carry the memory cards from the camera down canyon to the shop so I could stay up and keep shooting the afternoon trips. Once my own path became a big, sweeping circle leading back to the Midwest, this poem had to be in the collection. There are other lines or phrases that I'd been writing and revising for more than a decade.

There are a number of poems in the latter part of this collection which take their titles from writers who've worked on questions of culture and agriculture. Thoreau, Edward Abbey, Wendell Berry, there were a lot more of those; there were erasures and cut-ups pulled entirely from their work. I culled this down to the few that really related to this collection. There was a clunky serial poem about county fairs as a voyeuristic, celebratory, kitchy, and earnest celebration of rural life. It's heart relates to this collection, but I haven't figured it out yet. My county fair, The Great Geauga County Fair, is huge and one of the oldest in the nation. It's an incredible spectacle in so many ways.

Many of the poem titles in *Questions About Circulation* are bisected with a slash, such as "illusive / weeded." What is the significance of intentionally halving these titles?

When I am mindful, at my most open, I am always able to reflect on an image or experience and feel more than one thing. Often I find a complimentary thought or a contrasting one in the same material. The halving is a nudge toward plurality, for me as much as the reader. One problem with pastoral writing is when it is simple, when it is a postcard, or when it is removed from the reality of work, it becomes intentionally or accidentally dishonest. Many of these poems were once one long poem, each new section in someway trying to answer or challenge the previous. In a sense there's something dialectical about how I hope these sections speak to each other now. This is a feeling that I have a hard time finding prose to express. In "illusive / weeded," there is death and there is abundance, there are wild animals and kept animals, there is the enduring evidence of prior generations and the fleeting memories of childhood, there are absences or hollows and the landscape is thick with life. Sometimes the slash marks the interior childlike joy of being close to the land, of being muddy and sweaty, and exterior cultural pressures to find a life with higher cultural standing. This is true in a poem like "bootstraps / gooseberries." Perhaps the slashes mirror a mind/body dichotomy I hope to complicate. Not to trace too easy a metaphor, but I often want to follow the blood that flows from through our muscles and brings oxygen from the world to our brains.

Longer and longer lines appear throughout the collection, culminating in the title poem's prose block structure. How does this evolution of line length speak to the chapbook's concerns of growth and place?

I am always responding to what I've just written. Questioning it. Undermining it. Pushing it. If I am writing a lot of short, open-form poems, I answer them with longer poems with more of a distinct voice, measured stanzas, and other formal elements. In the first half of this collection I was really interested in sense and the presence of our bodies, in using this to invite others into these personal experiences. I felt the poems had to have a lot of space to create room for the reader. In later poems, I am pushing against my own quiet tendencies. By nature, I am an earnest and amenable person and I have to work to make direct statements. I borrow titles from lines written by Thoreau or Berry. Their direct, cutting statements refuse to let me write soft or easy pastoral or nature poetry. The influence of these voices pushes my own line length. They still have grounded imagery but their perspective allows for commentary and reflection on ideas that open the collection in a different direction. I see the chapbook as stepping from a very close, personal position, to a broader, more culturally-aware mode, and finally to the closing poem, which has the widest lens. The final poem offers eleven images, or statements, each trying to expand the metaphor of circulation. When this poem came, I finally knew how to pull the collection together. Without too much intention, a parallel developed between personal growth, artistic growth, and form.

Where does *Questions About Circulation* stand in the scope of your writing? Is this collection indicative of your poetry as a whole or do those poems hold a unique place in your personal catalogue?

C.D. Wright says in *Cooling Time* that "Every year the poem I most want to write, the poem that would in effect allow me to stop writing, changes shapes, changes directions." These were the poems I needed to write when I left home and when I came back. I had to make my peace with the different places I moved on from and those I came to live in. For someone who feels strongly connected to place, moving is both exciting and traumatic. It feels wonderful to see these poems in this shape.

While aspects of these poems will probably be at the core of everything I do, the poem I am most interested in writing today is different. I'm working as a teaching artist, conducting writing workshops in juvenile detention centers, refugee resettlement agencies, and with mental health support groups. I'm training undergraduates to do this work as well and the poem I want to write pierces through the humanity of these exchanges. We laugh so much, we cry so much, and I learn so much being in proximity with stories that couldn't be more different from the pastoral images in *Questions about Circulation*. Being open and present with these writers and these ideas means I am writing towards something different. At the same time, I'm back home, building a life as this community approaches a half century since the burning of the Cuyahoga River and the massacre of students on our campus at Kent State in 1970. My interests in the land and our history won't go away.

More to that point, will you ever return to the themes and concerns of this chapbook in future poems?

Almost certainly and certainly differently. For the most part, I walk or bike everywhere and that means the rare moments when I am left to my own curiosity are grounded in place. My childhood home sits at the top of the Cuyahoga watershed and my current home in Kent is a short walk from the river. Even when I am thinking about the story I've just heard from a Syrian refugee or a community member in recovery, I walk home beside a river with quick, dark waters and a long, dark history and there are connections. I have always seen myself as a rural, midwestern poet even when I lived in the West. Everyday, I confront the same world that shaped these poems.

What advice would you give to other poets writing about childhood, rural life, and connections to place?

Learn as much as you can about the history, geology, and the ecology of your place. Take your time, find the layers underneath your experience; find the writerly or psychological reasons why you come back to these memories. Let go of the poems that are for you and no one else. Yet, by all means keep writing those poems; that's one of the purest reasons to write—to make sense of our own experiences. Then hold those experiences up like a color slide against the lights of the larger world and focus on the ones you really want us to feel.

I'm not the kind of writer who ever felt a draw to big city life. I never thought I needed to go make it in New York. There are people writing New York poems better than I ever could and with real authority about that community. I loved my time out West. I love visiting New York, San Francisco, Portland—most any place—because I learn a lot by walking the streets and museums. Maybe that is part of the advice I should give: leave your place. Maybe you'll find your way back, maybe not, but you'll know it better. It feels rotten to make that suggestion, but I find myself wishing that for my students all the time.

What are you working on right now?

The poems that come from the teaching I am doing feel the most important. I come home from these conversations feeling an excited responsibility to challenge our narratives around immigration, addiction, mental health, and even education. I'm trying to figure out if these more overtly socially engaged poems can live side-by-side with questions of place and environment. I'm trying to speak in a voice that can hold and honor other voices. At the same time, my wife and I have been fixing up an old house, slowly and clumsily. There is another act to the questions in this collection about home and house and planet. I am also finding a rich vocabulary from these other kinds of work. These themes, social justice, home, and the environment, are linked and will become more so as the effects of climate change continue to assert themselves and are felt by our most vulnerable populations first. That's an essay, not a poem. I am also still bookish and always writing in response to whatever I am reading: books about symmetry, biographies of scientists, essays on architecture, articles on hoaxes and jokes of nature, histories of places I travel to. I've got love poems and political poems. I've got bicycle poems. I've got a cabinet of curiosities that I don't know what to do with. When I was at Colorado State a visiting writer told us that "a change is as good as a break," so when my writing gets stuck in one place I move to another, sometimes even to prose. Perhaps I've taken that advice too far. More than anything, with all these ideas in the air, given the strange state of our communities, I'm hopeful that I can write poems that will be useful to others. Poems that offer joy because the images are unfamiliar, or deeply familiar, or which offer questions that feel honest and urgent.

Charles Malone works with writers in the community around Northeastern Ohio through the Wick Poetry Center. He grew up in rural Geauga County, headed west to the Rockies, came back to the Great Lakes, and has loved all of it. He is the author of three collections of poetry: *After an Eclipse of Moths* (*Moonstone Arts*), *Questions About Circulation* (*Driftwood Press*), and *Working Hypothesis* (*Finishing Line Press*). He edited the anthology *A Poetic Inventory of Rocky Mountain National Park* with *Wolverine Farm Publishing* and *Light Enters the Grove: Exploring Cuyahoga Valley National Park through Poetry* (*Kent State University Press*). He lives in one of the most nurturing small towns for poets in Kent, Ohio.

"the house fire" *Hotel Amerika*, 2019.

"One Dozen Frozen Ponds" and "ruins" s*altfront: studies in human habit(at)*, 2018.

"prelude" and "illusive, weeded" *Sugar House Review*, Issue 6, 2012.

"Homing" *Phoebe*, Spring 2009.

OTHER DRIFTWOOD PRESS TITLES

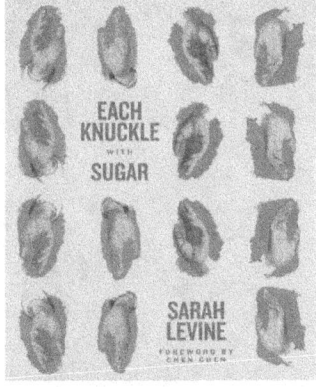

www.ingramcontent.com/pod-product-compliance
Lightning Source LLC
Chambersburg PA
CBHW052106110526
44591CB00013B/2379